CASH, The Fuel For Your Economic Engine

How 1+1+1=19

Gravitas Impact Monograph

JEFFREY A. REDMON
WITH ADAM SIEGEL

www.gravitasimpact.com

CASH, THE FUEL FOR YOUR ECONOMIC ENGINE.
Copyright© Gravitas Impact, 2020

FOREWORD

Community. What comes to mind when you say this word out loud? Family? Friends? Colleagues? Within Gravitas Impact, "Community" has a clear and compelling meaning based on our years of experience together...the collective care, intellect and impact of members who live and are inspired by similar core values and purpose.

It is out of this community that the concept of placing our "Coach at the Center" and sharing our "Networked Intellect" has arisen. These two concepts are the genesis of the Gravitas Impact community building an ongoing series of monographs addressing important business topics, relevant to leaders worldwide who value insights in a compact and actionable format, from a deeply experienced community of professionals on six continents.

In a global business world driven by the daily media, digital marketing and "business by best seller," we have chosen to tap into the richness and robustness of our community of seasoned business leaders, coaches and thought leaders to serve those who create, build and grow one of the fundamental building blocks of secure and successful societies: the executive leadership team in a business.

If you are reading this and see a need for insight into a business challenge, please reach out to us at mongraphs@gravitasimpact.com and we would be pleased to research and potentially address it with a future monograph.

– Keith Cupp, Founder Gravitas Impact Premium Coaches

Cash is not about finance, it is really an operational issue. We can only save nickels and dimes – the elements that ultimately add up to make a real difference in the business's bottom line – on the front lines, not in the executive offices.

Table of Contents:

Chapter 1: No CFO's Allowed..p1
  It's Not About Finance
  Back To Basics
  It's All About Operations

Chapter 2: Learning to Count..p7
  Time is Cash
  Your Cash Conversion Cycle
  Documenting Your Cash Conversion Cycle

Chapter 3: How 1+1+1=19...p13
  The Power of One
  Widgets R Us
  Leveraging The Power of One

Chapter 4: Finding Hidden Cash..p21
  Topline Revenue – Sales Cycle: Price
  Topline Revenue – Sales Cycle Volume
  Cost of Goods Sold
  Overhead Costs
  What's Your 1+1+1=19?

Chapter 5: Digging Deeper..p29
  Mapping Out Your Processes
  Shorten Time
  Eliminate Waste
  Eliminate Mistakes
  Change Your Business Model

Chapter 6: Fueling Your Engine..p39
  Cash, The Fuel For Your Economic Engine
  Power of One Financial Drivers
  You Don't Have To Go It Alone

CHAPTER 1: NO CFO'S ALLOWED

It's Not About Finance

No CFOs allowed. This sign is posted on the door for my 1+1+1=19 cash workshops, developed to show CEOs, owners and business leaders how to find cash within their companies rather than seeking outside capital to meet their needs and goals. Some of my best friends are accountants and CFOs, but cash—the fuel necessary to reduce debt, increase reserves, consistently fund payroll and expand—is not about finance.

While a company's CFO may be bonded for his fidelity in handling cash, he is not accountable for that cash until it is deposited in the bank. When accountability for cash is delegated to the CFO alone, a huge opportunity is squandered. It is critical that the business owner or CEO maintain accountability for cash. Why? There is no higher accountability for that owner or CEO than making sure the economic engine has the necessary fuel to thrive. Responsibility should be delegated down the chain of command as well (and we'll see why), but the owner or CEO must be the one leading the charge.

Accountability vs. Responsibility

ACCOUNTABILITY
- Only one person can be accountable
- Cannot be shared or delegated

RESPONSIBILITY
- Can include multiple team members
- Can be shared or delegated

Without cash, the economic engine will falter. In *How the Mighty Fall*, Jim Collins's sequel to *Good to Great*, Collins outlines how many of the companies profiled in his earlier book had failed, some in dramatic fashion. Collins notes that each strayed from the 'Hedgehog Concept', the idea that successful companies and their leaders are 'hedgehogs'—those who understood one big thing, namely where their skill and passion lie—rather than more scattered and inconsistent 'foxes'. But the biggest issue, plain and simple, was that they ran out of cash. They lost sight of their economic engine. Faltering cash was the earliest warning sign missed by these great companies, despite their teams of super smart executives.[1] How can we avoid the same outcome? It all comes down to cash.

Cash is not about finance. Rather, it is a necessary commodity input for every business, just as diesel fuel is for the farmer's tractor or aviation fuel for the pilot's aircraft. It is in every operational step that cash is earned, spent, delayed, wasted, saved and preserved. While most CFOs have established metrics, benchmarks and systems to count and account for cash, few companies use cash as a driving metric on their path to growth and vitality. Would you want to fly in a plane that did not have a fuel gauge? Cash needs to be on your economic engine's dashboard, available to the frontline teams who are generating and spending it—and to the company's leadership.

Back to Basics

Entrepreneurs often start their business using checkbook accounting. Is there cash in the bank to pay for today's payroll, rent and materials for the customer's order? These business owners are very aware that every decision they make either consumes or generates cash. Maybe they have a cash flow forecast for the month, quarter or even for the year, but they know their daily cash position too because they are in the trenches running their business, living their dream. As their business grows and thrives, the entrepreneur starts hiring, handing off jobs and tasks to others with specific skillsets. Then the big day comes when the "accounting function" is passed to a bookkeeper.

At this stage there is often no money for a chief financial officer, but CEO's finally have the resources to pay a person to count cash, send out invoices, collect receivables and pay bills. QuickBooks is often the platform used to cut checks, allocate costs to established buckets and provide monthly reports. The bookkeeper is the first step in separating the business owner from their full appreciation of cash. The bookkeeper is now responsible to watch the bank balance. However, our founder still signs checks and may hold a check here or there when they know there is not cash in the bank to cover it. At that point, cash is still king (or queen!).

When the business eventually thrives its way to hiring a Controller, and eventually a CFO, the transition is complete. The CEO no longer watches cash; rather the CFO is in charge of finance. But here's the problem: Cash is not about finance; it is really an operational issue. We can only save nickels and dimes —the elements that ultimately add up to make a real difference in the business's bottom line – on the front lines, not in the executive offices. That means we need to bring the CEO back to basics, to accountability for cash, and we need to operationalize it, to assure there is always fuel for the economic engine.

It's All About Operations

What part of operations does not use, make, delay or accelerate cash? Time is cash, mistakes are cash, inventory is cash waste is cash and so on. For example, let's start from the beginning: your marketing funnel. How do your marketing efforts attract customers? Would you rather pay $100 for the contact information of a ready, willing and able customer or put that same $100 toward a copy of the white pages with a million outdated business names, addresses and phone numbers—many of which lead nowhere? One could generate a sale tomorrow while the other starts a long process to filter, find and qualify a customer interested in interacting with a salesperson. Does your decision change if you need 100 customers? How about 10 million?

Processes take time and cost cash. The longer this marketing process takes, the more cash in the bank is delayed. When your marketing is not hyper-focused on attracting your ideal core customer, your company must spend cash to filter and sort the qualified customers from the vast number of suspects caught in your indiscriminate net. We need to start visualizing dollar bills slipping out the door—or through the walls or floorboards—with every passing moment. One business owner I worked with remarked he wanted to be there when they tore down his old building because he knew at least $250,000 had fallen through the cracks.

Do you know the cash value of every day, hour and minute? Does a daylong delay cost your business $10, $100 or $1,000? When I was chairman of our local hospital board, I found that it was taking ninety-eight days to collect on each bill they issued. Each day it took to collect those invoices cost that hospital real cash in the bank: $200,000 a day. Without that cash in the bank, it was struggling to pay its bills. When we eliminated invoicing mistakes to the insurance companies and shortened the collection time to fifty days, covering our bills was no longer a problem—there was plenty to go around. Talk about fueling your economic engine!

This is just one example of the tremendous success I've seen companies achieve when they started seeing every operational element of their business as cash, and began making an effort to hold onto more of it. That's what we'll do here. I'll show you how every aspect of your business can be represented by cash, how to better manage it, and what a difference that makes. I'll also show you the value of teaching your team members about the importance of cash, so they can begin to count and manage the cash associated with their roles. Their knowledge and ability to manage their roles successfully will bring security, as better cashflow brings security to a business.

When everyone involved in your operation can see piles of dollar bills, pesos, or euros associated with every function, you will be on your way to maximizing your business's cash.

But first, you need to learn how to count.

KEY POINTS:

It's Not About Finance: Cash is not about finance. Rather, it is a necessary commodity input for every business, just as diesel fuel is for the farmer's tractor or aviation fuel for the pilot's aircraft. It is in every operational step that cash is earned, spent, delayed, wasted, saved and preserved.

Back To Basics: Cash is not about finance; it is really an operational issue. We can only save nickels and dimes —the elements that ultimately add up to make a real difference in the business's bottom line – on the front lines, not in the executive offices. That means we need to bring the CEO back to basics, to accountability for cash, and we need to operationalize it, to assure there is always fuel for the economic engine.

It's All About Operations: Do you know the cash value of every day, hour and minute?

CHAPTER 2: LEARNING TO COUNT

Time is Cash

Before we can learn to count, we need to know exactly what we are counting. Your business may operate in US dollars or Australian ones, euros, pesos or even bitcoin, but for our purposes, the currency doesn't matter—all of that counts as cash. Seems pretty straightforward, but most companies aren't counting it!

They're good at tabulating the number of people on their teams, products sold, customers booked and inventory on the shelves. But what about how long it takes to attract a qualified buyer? How long it takes to close a sale? Or how long it takes to make or turn around the product after it is sold? What about the time it takes to deliver that product, or how long it takes to send a bill or receive payment? These metrics aren't often considered, and yet they are critical. In fact, each is a component of your Cash Conversion Cycle (CCC)[2].

The Cash Conversion Cycle:

In its simplest form, your Cash Conversion Cycle is the number of days it takes from the day you start spending money to acquire an account until your company receives cash from the sale.

The day you open your doors for business—and often before then—you are spending cash. You must pay the rent, utilities, phone and internet bills. You may have bought furniture and equipment and hired employees. All of these expenses require cash, and all of them occur before the first sale—and certainly before you earn that first dollar from sales. That old adage remains true: time is money. That's why the Cash Conversion Cycle is so important—it focuses on the time it takes to collect cash from your customers. The faster you recognize that cash is a critical operational metric that everyone should be counting, the sooner you will maximize the fuel for your economic engine.

Remember the hospital we discussed in Chapter 1? It sends out $200,000 in invoices per day. As such, every day it takes to collect that cash means $200,000 less in the bank. How long does it take for you to collect on your invoices? Your accountant or CFO calls this Accounts Receivable aging, or A/R aging. When I joined the hospital's board, it took an average of 98 days from the day the invoice was sent out to the day the hospital received payment. What took so long? Most of these invoices were sent to health insurance companies that had strict rules about documentation. If an invoice failed to follow a single rule, the invoice was returned unpaid. Worse, if an invoice failed multiple documentation rules, the insurance company would note just one of them and return the claim unpaid, noting the error. That error might be corrected, only to be returned again for another documentation issue—the process repeating again and again until every single issue was addressed. You can just imagine the delays that created!

But by implementing a diligent system of review and documentation compliance, the number of returned claims was significantly reduced, ultimately shortening the A/R aging from 98 days to 50 days. With each day equating to $200,000, shaving five days off the process meant $1 Million in the bank. Trimming 48 days equaled a whopping $9.6 Million. It's a lot easier to pay bills with cash in the bank than with days of A/R aging. Of course, banks might loan you money against your quality accounts receivable, but when you've already collected on those invoices you don't have to worry about that—including any interest charges that borrowing may entail.

Your Cash Conversion Cycle

With that in mind, let's take a closer look at your Cash Conversion Cycle. Our CFO friends often focus on the period beginning with the day money is spent on inventory to produce a product until the day cash is received from the sale of the finished product. But in reality, the Cash Conversion Cycle starts the moment you spend money to acquire an account.

The Marketing/Sales Cycle: Your Cash Conversion Cycle starts when you spend money on marketing to prospective customers. Your marketing cycle ends when you turn over qualified leads to your sales team, and the sales cycle begins. Sales cycles range from the instantaneous online point-and-click to the multi-year government or industry mega-contract. Regardless of the size of each sale, your marketing and sales cycles take time. The shorter that period of time is, the faster you can put your cash in the bank. This is why referrals from existing satisfied customers are so valuable.

Make/Production and Inventory Cycle: Your sales team has closed the sale with a signed contract. Now, how long will it take to deliver the goods? Do you need to order the raw materials, wait for delivery and then produce the products, or do you have finished goods on the shelf ready to be shipped out when ordered? Regardless of the product or service you provide, it takes time and money to move that sale from an order to cash in the bank.

Delivery Cycle: Once your product is made, how do you get it to the customer? Do you send it electronically, or ship it? This piece is governed by yet another period of time and pile of money that separates you from your customer's order and cash in the bank.

Billing & Payment Cycle: You have attracted a prospect, converted a customer, made the product and delivered it. Now it's time to bill and collect the cash (assuming you don't collect at the point of sale). This is yet another hurdle of time and expense separating you from your cash in the bank.

Documenting Your Cash Conversion Cycle

So, how much cash does each of these cycles mean to you? That depends on how much time they take. Let's say your annual sales are $3,600,000. You are selling $900,000 each quarter, $300,000 a month, and $10,000 each day in a 360-day year. You can break down your own sales to determine cash per day using the following formula.

FORMULAS	EXAMPLE	YOUR COMPANY
Annual Sales	$3,600,000	
Quarterly = Annual/4	$900,000	
Monthly = Annual/12	$300,000	
Daily = Annual/# Days	$10,000	

Now, let's break things down a little further. Consider the various cycles in your business, and determine how many days each takes. Convert days to cash using your previous answer.

CYCLE	EXAMPLE		YOUR COMPANY	
	DAYS	CASH	DAYS	CASH
Marketing	30	$300,000		
Sales	10	$100,000		
Production	7	$70,000		
Delivery	5	$50,000		
Billing & Payment	30	$300,000		
Cash Conversion Cycle	**82**	**$820,000**		

Our hypothetical company uses $820,000 of cash between the day it starts spending money on marketing until it collects its first dollar from sales. What are your numbers? If you can shorten your marketing or sales cycle by just one day, you put one day of cash in the bank one day sooner. Consider creative solutions to shorten the Cash Conversion Cycle. Instead of charging monthly for your products or services, what if you charged up front, with additional charges occurring on an annual basis? Your billing and payment cycle could very well end up being -360 days, and you would then be using your customer's cash to fuel your economic engine.

There are 3 primary ways to improve your Cash Conversion Cycle:

1. Reduce Cycle Times

2. Eliminate Mistakes

3. Improve your Business Model

An important note here: It is better to make your best guess at each cycle length of time, with your team's input, than waiting to be precise! Get moving on educating, estimating and improving your CCC. Estimate each sub-cycle and begin to improve it, while the team determines how to more precisely measure it with metrics on a weekly basis. You can download your complimentary Gravitas Impact *Cash Conversion Cycle Worksheet* at **www.GravitasImpact.com/FuelYourEngine** and begin to outline strategies for accelerating your Cash Flow now!

The faster you can put cash in the bank, the more cash you will have to pay bills, fund growth, and take advantage of opportunities without having to rely on loans or investment capital.

KEY POINTS:

Time Is Cash: In its simplest form, your Cash Conversion Cycle is the number of days it takes from the day you start spending money to acquire an account until your company receives cash from the sale.

3 Ways to Accelerate Your Cash Conversion Cycle:

1. Reduce Cycle Times

2. Eliminate Mistakes

3. Improve your Business Model

You can download your complimentary Gravitas Impact *Cash Conversion Cycle Worksheet* at **www.GravitasImpact.com/FuelYourEngine** and begin to outline strategies for accelerating your Cash Flow now!

CHAPTER 3: HOW 1+1+1=19

The Power of One

If the Cash Conversion Cycle drills down on how to accelerate your cash flow, the Power of One focuses on how to refine it. The concept, popularized in business by Alan Miltz and Jos Milner of Cash Flow Story, is quite simple: How might your cash flow improve if you increased one internal operational outcome by just one percent?[3] The effect is probably more significant than you expect. And with seven financial variables you can adjust to make that one percent shift, you can have a significant impact on cash.

Power of One Drivers:

- Price

- Volume

- Cost of Goods Sold (COGS)

- Accounts Receivables (A/R)

- Accounts Payable (A/P)

- Inventory (Turns)

- Overhead Expense

With minor tweaks to these drivers—increasing or decreasing to improve their outcomes—the Power of One sends a much higher percentage increase to your bottom-line cash position, often called net income. On a technical note, your CFO or accountant includes some non-cash items in your net income but each of the Power of One drivers impact net income as cash.

With the Power of One, one plus one plus one can equal nineteen: 1+1+1=19. No funny math, just simple arithmetic—as the following income statement demonstrates.

Widgets R Us

Widgets R Us sells the best widgets money can buy. They sell $1 Million in widgets each year. It costs them $500,000 to produce these widgets (COGS). Their rent, utilities and other overhead expenses are $400,000, leaving them with $100,000 in bottom-line net income cash. You can add or subtract zeros for your business, but your income statement—regardless of its complexity—can be reduced to these simple elements, no CFO needed.

VARIABLES	EXAMPLE	YOUR COMPANY
Sales/Price	$1,000,000	
COGS	$500,000	
Overhead	$400,000	
Net Income	$100,000	

Now, let's see what happens when we increase price—and therefore sales—by one percent. That one percent increase results in a $10,000 bump in total sales. Might your market allow for that 1 percent price increase?

VARIABLES	EXAMPLE	+1%
Sales/Price	$1,000,000	$10,000

In the production of widgets, a savings of just one percent would add up to $5,000. That might come in the form a savings on the cost of raw materials; it might come in cutting the cost of labor by improving efficiency—the opportunities are endless. And remember, the changes don't have to be major. We are looking for those slight improvements, or maybe a series of savings, that add up to one percent.

VARIABLES	EXAMPLE	-1%
COGS	$500,000	$5,000

Who is best suited to uncover these savings? Those on the front lines, doing the job. Every day, they see the pile of waste that builds up, or the inefficiencies in the system. Most of the time, those in the corner office upstairs assume it's just a few dollars—no big deal in our $1 Million business. We'll see if that's true.

Widgets R Us's overhead is $400,000, so one percent is just $4,000 over the course of a year. That's just $333.33 in savings a month we are looking for. How might you reduce your overhead costs by just one percent?

VARIABLES	EXAMPLE	-1%
Overhead	$400,000	$4,000

As we add up these one percent improvements, the impact on our $100,000 net income is $19,000 cash, or a 19% increase in net income. 1+1+1=19!!!

VARIABLES	EXAMPLE	+/- 1%
Sales/Price	$1,000,000	$10,000
COGS	$500,000	$5,000
Overhead	$400,000	$4,000
Net Income	$100,000	$19,000

Widgets R Us does not exist, but these facts do—and they remain true for countless businesses across the world. You don't need a CFO to count total annual sales, what it costs to produce those widgets, and the overhead of the business. Every business sells something that cost money to make or deliver, with overhead to generate and spend cash. What is your 19%?

I've coached over 100 businesses through this exercise, and have never seen less than a ten percent increase to net income. In some cases, the increase was over 80%. Fill in your numbers to see what kind of outcome you could achieve.

VARIABLES	YOUR COMPANY	+/- 1%
Sales/Price		
COGS		
Overhead		
Net Income		

How 1+1+1=19, A Client Story:

I've coached multiple companies through the How 1+1+1=19 Worksheet. It's such a practical tool that brings about rapid cash flow impact.

One example was an education lead generation company dealing with one of the major search engines – it was the biggest spend item and most critical supplier they have. They were on tight payment terms as a standard. Once they walked through the activity, they implemented a negotiation strategy that was able to push out Accounts Payable days by a number of weeks. This led to a major improvement in cash flow of almost $80,000 in the first month alone.

Another was an industry certification company who went through this exercise and found that they had not reviewed pricing in more than 7 years! Excited about the prospect of a unilateral and significant price increase, they gathered themselves and carefully segmented their customer base and product offerings. Based on the market research, and competitor analysis, they found that some products needed to be reduced, whilst others could be increased significantly. The outcome was an average price increase accepted by the market of more than five percent across the board!

- Adam Siegel, Gravitas Impact Coach
Melbourne, Australia

Leveraging The Power of One

Our *How 1+1+1=19 Worksheet* is a great tool to help you find your hidden cash and see the bottom-line impact for your business. You can download this complimentary tool at **www.GravitasImpact.com/FuelYourEngine.** CEO, tread lightly here: If you start by taking charge and immediately present your ideas—no matter how good—you'll have diminished the expectations on your team to contribute. It's best to stand back and let others get the ball rolling. Let them know, too, that there are no bad ideas, that nothing is too big or too small to be worthwhile. Just get ideas on the table. If they miss something you've already recognized, consider whether you can get them to see it with a question, helping them look for the next right answer.

One technique I have found helpful to assure full participation is to use 3x5 index cards. Rather than just putting ideas on newsprint or a whiteboard, have each team member pause and write their ideas on a 3x5 index card. Then, go around the room, asking each team member to share an idea from their card and put it on the newsprint or whiteboard. Have them cross out any repeats, and write down any new ideas triggered during the conversation. Keep going around the room until all new ideas are on the table.

Post-it® notes also work well for this purpose. Each person puts their ideas on a Post-it® —one idea per Post-it®. Members then place their Post-it® on large sheets of newsprint. Duplicates can be stacked, and ideas can be moved around and grouped as necessary. Why are notecards and Post-it® notes preferable to newsprint and white board methods, in which employees share and document their ideas en masse? These techniques give your introverts time to process, and keep your extroverts—or most vocal team members—from dominating the discussion. The purpose here is to get ideas, ideas, ideas, and to do that everyone needs a chance to contribute.

The next step is to record all of those brilliant ideas on your worksheet. As you record each one, determine the annual total dollar impact implementing that particular idea could have. Not quite sure how to harness the Power of One in your operation? We've got you covered. Next, we will explore where you might find those hidden dollars—the nickels in the niches—that you can use to fuel your economic engine.

KEY POINTS:

The Power of One: How might your cash flow improve if you increased one internal operational outcome by just one percent?

Widgets R Us: Widgets R Us does not exist, but these facts do—and they remain true for countless businesses across the world. You don't need a CFO to count total annual sales, what it costs to produce those widgets, and the overhead of the business. Every business sells something that cost money to make or deliver, with overhead to generate and spend cash. What is your 19%?

Leveraging the Power of One: Our *How 1+1+1=19 Worksheet* is a great tool to help you find your hidden cash and see the bottom-line impact for your business. You can download this complimentary tool at **www.GravitasImpact.com/FuelYourEngine.**

CHAPTER 4: FINDING HIDDEN CASH

So, where is all that extra cash in your operation? It's time to dig a little deeper and find out. Grab your How 1+1+1=19 Worksheet and follow along!

Topline Revenue – Sales Cycle: Price

The simplest way to increase topline sales by one percent is to increase price by one percent. For Widgets R Us, one percent of $1 Million in annual sales translates to a $10,000 increase in topline sales. No increase in cost of goods sold, same number of widgets being sold—just an extra $10,000 added to those invoices over the course of a year.

If Widgets R Us sells $1 Million in widgets annually at $1.00 apiece, the one percent increase brings the price of their widgets up to $1.01. Can you imagine Widgets R Us' customers heading elsewhere due to a penny increase in price? I don't think so.

There's another truth that factors into this equation: Most of us underprice what we sell—and that gives us the wiggle room to charge a little more. If you sell gasoline at a corner with four other gas stations, the market may not allow you to increase your gas price by a penny a gallon, but most of us can squeeze another one percent out of our market. Consider whether your customers might be amenable to paying a little more for the great product or service you provide.

Topline Revenue – Sales Cycle: Volume

This next concept may seem a little more complicated, but I assure you that you don't need a finance degree to figure out how increased volume affects your bottom line—perhaps just a bit more concentration. So, bear with me and put your thinking cap on; we're about to discuss volume.

Each time Widgets R Us sells one more widget for $1.00, it costs an additional $0.50 to produce it. So, the full $1.00 does not fall to the bottom line, but an extra $0.50 does. It may not seem like it, but those fifty-cent pieces add up as you push for bottom-line impact. And the ways to increase sales volume are only limited by your imagination.

We can look to Costco's business model for a clear example. The wholesale giant requires you to buy three bottles of ketchup rather than just the one you can buy at Walmart. The cost per bottle may be less than you'd pay at Walmart, but the fact that you have to buy three of them at a time automatically increases sales volume with every purchase. Essentially, they are focused on selling more to current customers.

Another company I coached found serious value in the same strategy. Despite a dozen initiatives to increase sales, their sales had been flat for three years. Using the Gravitas Impact Growth Roadmap planning process, they determined the one thing that would have the biggest impact on sales was to make more sales to current customers.

With this information in hand, they dropped all the other shiny strategies that distracted from this focused sales priority: to make more sales to current customers.

When they honed in on what they had to do, they saw real results: In year 1, topline sales increased 25%. Year 2 saw another 30% increase, and year 3 another 23%. Their sales went from $8 million to $10 million to $13 million, then $16 million—doubling in just three years. Of course, their cost of goods sold (COGS) increased, but ultimately they added just a single person to their staff (which contributed to overhead) while making twice the sales. The bottom-line cash impact was huge.

Your *How 1+1+1=19 Worksheet*:

With your team, brainstorm what your company might do to increase sales. For example, for items that increase volume, subtract your current cost of goods sold to determine your bottom-line impact. Assign responsibility and calculate the annual cash impact for each action. What is the percentage change of your topline sales?

Cost of Goods Sold

Next up in our search for hidden cash: cost of goods sold (COGS). What can your business do to decrease the cost of production by one percent? Whether you sell a widget or provide a service, there is a cost to providing what you sell.

Physical items require raw materials, take time and labor to produce, and often need to be packaged and delivered. If you provide clients with an online service, those production costs remain: There may be equipment, support services, a call center, bandwidth expense and more. If you run a company that provides professional services—from law to plumbing— you've got to pay for the professionals who provide those services. Your COGS may be small compared to how much you charge for your service, but that doesn't mean that cost can't be examined and reduced.

Even seconds matter. One of my clients ran a business that assembled small parts for the auto industry. She would often suggest that she sold and managed seconds. If they assembled 10,000 pieces and could save one second per item, that was 10,000 seconds, 167 minutes, or 2.78 hours saved. If every employee hour costs $36, including wages, taxes, and benefits, that one second saved per piece translates to a $100 savings on a production run of 10,000 pieces.

What about the costs associated with running your business? Inputs matter too. A trucking company client used a forward purchase contract for his trucking fleet to save $5,000 a week on his fuel bill. $5,000 times fifty-two weeks is a whopping $260,000 in cash available to grow the business or put in shareholders' pockets. Where can your team find that hidden cash in your production cycle?

Your *How 1+1+1=19 Worksheet:*

With your team, brainstorm ideas to save money on your cost of goods or services sold. Where can you save a second, minute, an hour, or even days? Where can you eliminate waste, mistakes, or change your process to save cash Assign responsibility and calculate the annual cash impact for each action. What are the savings as a percentage of your cost of goods sold?

Overhead Costs

Every business has overhead—that is, the cost of opening the doors, regardless of how many widgets you might sell on any given day. Overhead includes rent, utilities, taxes, insurance, cleaning services, your bookkeeping and payroll staff or service and more—the list goes on and on. Like our other processes, overhead seems to grow over time without constant vigilance.

The goal in this process is not to reduce quality—we can always find cheaper paper towels—but to find something that costs less and works just as effectively for your business. You may decide a lesser-quality product meets your needs, but finding cash without sacrificing quality requires a deeper analysis. As you go about this process, nothing should be off limits. My city had just elected a new mayor, and he came to that office looking to minimize the cost of government operations without affecting the quality of services offered. Government is a business too, with a Cash Conversion Cycle and processes that can be further optimized.

He assigned a person to champion each line of the expense report and asked everyone to look for savings opportunities in their area. One expense line was insurance, with an annual cost of $155,000 per year. The champion was reluctant to make any adjustments, as he had just rebid insurance with their agent of many years. The mayor was insistent: no sacred cows; each line would be reviewed.

After a process that took twenty-two staff hours, the city secured identical insurance coverage at a savings of $35,000: a 22.6% savings with absolutely no impact on quality. They saved a total of $1,590 for each hour they spent reviewing. I don't care what city employees make; I can assure you no one is making over $1,500 per hour. Without any reduction in the quality of city services, the city now has an extra $35,000 to spend on other functions of government. What could you change to save on overhead?

Your *How 1+1+1=19 Worksheet:*

Repeat the brainstorming process from before with your overhead costs. Assign responsibility and calculate the annual cash impact for each action. What is the saving as a percentage of your overhead?

What's Your 1+1+1=19?

With the brainstorming of your topline sales, COGS and overhead combined, what is your percentage increase for net income? Insert the annual cash impact of each and do the math. What is the cash impact in your net income? Take that dollar amount and divide it by your initial net income, multiply by 100, and you have your 19%.

Through this exercise, your team will start to understand that you do not need to increase sales by 20% to increase the bottom line by 20%. Not all of these ideas will pan out or make sense in the morning, but you should have a list that has substantial impact. Take what works and toss the rest. Rinse and repeat as often as you like; you will find additional cash every time you stop to examine your process—I guarantee it. Make this exercise a part of our regular business continuous improvement process. Many companies run this exercise quarterly.

I once met a CEO who believed her organization didn't have the cash to cover the cost of Gravitas Impact coaching services. I told her that if she'd give me the time with her team—just an hour or so over lunch—we would find it. In that short period of time, they uncovered more than enough to pay for the organization's coaching fees.

When I do this exercise in a workshop, I guarantee that participants will find cash at least twenty times the cost of the workshop or I'll give them their money back. I would give them an hour of my time—just as I did with that CEO—to find 20 times their investment. I've never had a taker.

KEY POINTS:

Topline Revenue: Sales Cycle - Price: The simplest way to increase topline sales by one percent is to increase price by one percent.

Topline Revenue – Sales Cycle: Volume: Focus your sales priority: Make more sales to current customers.

Cost of Goods Sold: Your COGS may be small compared to how much you charge for your service, but that doesn't mean that cost can't be examined and reduced.

Overhead Costs: The goal in this process is not to reduce quality, but to find something that costs less and works just as effectively for your business.

What's Your 1+1+1=19? With the brainstorming of your topline sales, COGS and overhead combined, what is your percentage increase for net income? Make this exercise a part of our regular business continuous improvement process.

CHAPTER 5: DIGGING DEEPER

Mapping Out Your Processes

To really dig into other places where cash can hide, let's take a deeper look at your Cash Conversion Cycle from Chapter 1.

Whatever your business, your Cash Conversion Cycle is driven by your processes. You must attract and close customers, a process that includes marketing efforts and sales systems to close deals. You've got to produce your product and deliver it. You've got to invoice those customers, collect your cash, and pay your own bills. With that in mind, sketch out a map of your key processes. Keep it super high level—no need to get into the operational details here; our only goal is to identify those overarching process functions. We can dig deeper later.

Now, determine who is accountable for each of those functions. Next to each function, list the initials of the person accountable for it. In order to ensure accountability, make sure you're just listing one person. That person becomes accountable for cash within that function. They may delegate responsibility for activities or tasks, but this person shoulders the accountability.

You already know that the nickels are in the niches of your process. Hidden in the corners of every process you just listed are opportunities to find cash. Some of the best ways to find that extra cash are shortening times, eliminating waste and mistakes and changing your process or business model. Let's take a closer look at each one.

Shorten Time

By now, I hope you have come to appreciate that time is truly money, literally dollars ticking away with every passing second. Shortening time either saves labor expenses or accelerates the time it takes for cash to find its way into your bank.

When my client that doubled sales in three years worked to improve their processes to find more cash, they discovered a bottleneck in their production cycle: a single employee. She could process each order in half an hour, for a total of 16 orders processed per day. Seeing that sales would soon exceed her capacity to keep up, the company reviewed the system in hopes of finding ways to shorten the time it took to process each order. When they dug in, though, they found that many of the systems that could be altered to save time actually occurred around this employee.

For one, members of the sales team often made mistakes or left out key information as they completed order forms, requiring that those order forms be returned to them so they could fill in what they had missed. Thus, the first adjustment the company made was with the sales team, instituting processes to ensure forms were completed more accurately the first time around. This saved time to process each order.

Next, they found that, on occasion, orders were placed for items that were actually out of stock. Better integrating the inventory control system with the sales process could help avoid that issue, ensuring that items wouldn't run dangerously low before more inventory was ordered.

After that process was squared away, they reviewed the entirety of the ordering process from start to finish, cutting out any steps that weren't essential across various departments. And lastly, with the knowledge that the goal was increasing sales among current customers—and that they would thus be managing more sales per ticket rather than more individual orders—they realized that another set of hands part-time would be enough to handle the influx. That way, they could get through their processes faster without dialing up overhead costs in a major way.

Eliminate Waste

Waste is ubiquitous in our society. Our trash containers are a microcosm of our world—filled to the brim with excess. And sometimes waste is quite literally draining your cash.

I had a restaurant client where the manager would open a trash bag at every single one of his all-team meetings. The team would take note of mistakes that had ended up in the trash: food that customers regularly left behind, good silverware or plates that were inadvertently discarded during the dinner rush. No matter how often he had the team examine the trash, there was always avoidable waste in those bags.

Chances are the same is true for your business, no matter what kind of operation you have: waste exists—and that it's costing you cash.

A paper processing plant that found a creative—and lucrative—way to cut down on their waste. The plant produced a slurry of wet tree sap for years—a waste byproduct that had to be disposed of to the tune of millions of dollars each year.

To figure out how to cut down on waste and its corresponding cost, the company hired a scientist to help them determine what to do with their pesky byproduct. The scientist showed them how to reprocess the slurry to extract its natural sugars, which could then be sold to other industries. Thus, the company not only cut down on the money being lost in the disposal process; they also found a way to make their waste profitable! Is there a similar solution lurking in your trash?

Eliminate Mistakes

Mistakes are often a big contributor to waste. Whether in terms of stuff or time—the product that must be discarded because of faulty packaging, or a sales form that must be redone because a number is wrong—mistakes cost cash.

Remember our friends who doubled their sales in three years? They found forms were frequently incomplete and included mistakes, resulting in significant processing delays. When they made a concerted effort to fill out every form completely and correctly the first time, they saved time. An initiative led by the person accountable for that function, of course—they were able to keep more cash in the bank.

I also worked with a company that produced fasteners for the automotive industry. They became obsessed with eliminating mistakes for the sake of their bottom line—and saw outstanding results. Their commitment to quality was nothing short of spectacular. Every step in the production cycle was engineered to prioritize quality and eliminate mistakes. One year, they delivered 600 million parts without a single return—not one mistake had been made. While the quality process they had built included added expenses for the business, the amount they saved by putting an end to returns and ensuring customer satisfaction and loyalty would be hard to measure.

But it's not just mistakes that could be leaking cash, it may be the processes or models you've developed.

Change Your Business Model

How you sell your products is a cash opportunity worth exploring. Here's a classic business model story in which a small shift made a big difference for the company's bottom line. A local bird feed store began struggling when a new big box store opened up across the street. Why? That big box store sold bird feed in fifty-pound bags at a much cheaper price than the independent bird feed store.

The small bird feed store's owners knew they had to do something to keep up. So, they changed their business model to offer customers a fifty-pound option at an equally affordable rate. But then, they took it a step further, improving upon that box store's model: customers could take as much or as little of the fifty pounds as they wanted at a time. The business would store the rest. That way, the customer could avoid the chance of rodents attacking that fifty-pound bag in their garage, or forgo worrying about where to put it. As they required more, they could come in and get more of their fifty-pound account. It was as simple as that.

While this business model change lowered the price per pound, it accelerated their Cash Conversion Cycle. The fifty pounds was paid for on that first visit, which meant the bird feed store had cash in the bank. This pivot also had an unexpected outcome. When folks came in to pick up their birdseed, they often bought something else. Those impulse purchases were an added bonus to the business's topline sales.

Your business model likely has room for improvement, but your processes deserve your review as well.

Why do you do it that way? When I pose this question, the vast majority of the time I get the following answer: "That's the way we have always done it."

Humans like routine. Rarely do we stop doing anything; we simply add layers of process on top of what we have always done. Over time, our processes often morph. They become cluttered. We solved a problem when we added that extra step, but we don't step back and look at whether we could do things altogether differently, saving ourselves more time or energy—and thus, money. Don't be afraid to examine your processes. You never know what you'll find—and how much cash it might translate to.

Not all companies have the opportunity to change their business model in transformational ways—but when those opportunities do come along, they can really pay off. One of my clients pioneered secure internet connections, which they sold to the health care industry. Prior to my client's innovation, medical records couldn't be transmitted over the internet. Almost all health reimbursement claims were submitted over a DSL modem at a cost of about $30 per month.

When my client came on the scene with their superior service, it didn't come nearly as cheap: they charged about $1,000 per month. A national venture capital firm invested in my client. They were able to borrow several million dollars to buy the primary dial-up DSL modem service with which they were competing. With that move, they retired the dial-up service, and replaced it with their offering, creating over $100 million in free cash. Soon after, my client was able to sell for an impressive $550 million. It was a big process shift, but it was certainly worthwhile.

Cash Conversion Cycle, A Client Story:

I worked with a major custom home builder in Australia looking into one strategic initiative that aimed to increase and accelerate their cash flow using two of the key elements in the Cash Conversion Cycle Worksheet strategy: Shortening Time, and Eliminating Waste and Mistakes.

Shorten Time: They collected 90% of their cash through five progress payments across their homes' construction. This is what we considered the "Delivery Cycle" component of the Cash Conversion Cycle. The quicker they were able to complete the home, the sooner they would be able to realise and collect their cash. Their critical number for productivity was measured by an industry standard known as "dollars of revenue per day".

For context, this organization was able to illustrate the difference between having a productive supervisor who could generate on average $3,000 per day, versus an unproductive supervisor who would generate $1,100 per day. Across thousands of homes, the size of the prize for shortening cycle times was substantial!

Another adjustment we were able to make was implementing an quality assurance program that would reduce construction time and in particular time spent on re-work. This involved living one of the company values (they called them "Golden Rules") called "get it right first time". This was applied internally and was rolled out across all external suppliers and contractors.

The addition of a Quality Assurance Team that worked in collaboration (not opposition) to the Construction Team was also critical. They would provide ongoing feedback about repetitive quality issues and mistakes they were finding, and then educated Construction Staff as to how to mitigate these issues and errors. These changes reduced construction times by more than 35% on average.

Eliminate Waste: The company also ran a "LEAN construction blitz" across all 4 parts of the Cash Conversion Cycle. They did this with cross-functional teams along with the inclusion of select suppliers and trades. Over $10 Million in "waste" was identified for reduction, using Lean Construction principles. Beyond just physical waste, this included reduction in excess "specifications" of lumber/timber and other building materials, the minimizing of drafting and/or estimating errors that led to excess product on site, clarification of product usage guidelines to enable greater accuracy, maximizing the use and efficiency of trades, reducing the overlap of Construction Supervisor territories, elimination of non-productive site visits and return-trips, and revising the parameters for site set-up and cleanliness.

These changes had a multi-million dollar benefit to the business. From a physical waste perspective, on-site bins went from being emptied between five and seven times per project to three – saving $120 per bin due to lowering site waste in total. Across thousands of sites, this was a significant saving.

Eliminate Mistakes: As shared previously, the company implemented a increased quality assurance processes across the business. Particular focus was on 5 key construction milestones across the home build. The two most significant areas of focus were the foundation/slab and the frame stages. If these two milestones were completed to the desired quality, there is a far greater likelihood that remainder of the project would flow smoother.

It was agreed that work on that home build was to stop to allow for the Quality Assurance program's on-site quality checks to take place and any rectifications to be actioned prior to the job continuing. Even with these additional pauses, the Quality Assurance program was instrumental in reducing construction time downs to as fast as 16 weeks for a custom-built single story (from 24 weeks), 22 weeks (from 32 weeks) for a custom-built double story home. And, as we all know, time is money. This massive shift in production times through eliminating mistakes had a multi-million dollar impact on company profitability.

Using two of the disciplines of the Cash Conversion Cycle tool led to the creation of best-in-class processes and outcomes across the Australian home building industry, with sizable benefits for the company itself.

- Adam Siegel, Gravitas Impact Coach
Melbourne, Australia

KEY POINTS:

Mapping Out Your Processes: You already know that the nickels are in the niches of your process. Hidden in the corners of every process you just listed are opportunities to find cash. Some of the best ways to find that extra cash are shortening times, eliminating waste and mistakes and changing your process or business model.

Shorten Time: By now, I hope you have come to appreciate that time is truly money, literally dollars ticking away with every passing second. Shortening time either saves labor expenses or accelerates the time it takes for cash to find its way into your bank.

Eliminate Waste: Waste is ubiquitous in our society. Our trash containers are a microcosm of our world—filled to the brim with excess. And sometimes waste is quite literally draining your cash.

Eliminate Mistakes: Mistakes are often a big contributor to waste. Whether in terms of stuff or time—the product that must be discarded because of faulty packaging, or a sales form that must be redone because a number is wrong—mistakes cost cash.

Change Your Business Model: Not all companies have the opportunity to change their business model in transformational ways—but when those opportunities do come along, they can really pay off.

CHAPTER 6: FUELING YOUR ENGINE

Cash, The Fuel For Your Economic Engine

Every business is fueled by cash. Periods of rapid growth often require additional cash, which is used to fund the production of stuff to sell before the cash is received from the growing business. Some take investment dollars and grow substantially without generating positive net income. They just burn through it—in some cases sending millions, even billions, up in smoke.

For most of us, if our business does not generate the cash we need to operate, we borrow money from the bank. Some of us have unfortunately used credit cards to make up for our cash shortfall.

But in many cases, it doesn't have to be that way. Using the *Cash Conversion Cycle Worksheet,* I outlined how you can accelerate, and increase, your cash flow through shortening time, eliminating waste and mistakes and changing your business process or model. As the Power of One concept illustrates, even an incremental increase or decrease in your financial variables can affect your bottom line. Through the *How 1+1+1=19* exercise, I demonstrated that you can—and should—find cash within your operations to fuel your economic engine.

I've focused on three of the biggest financial drivers: sales through price and volume, cost of goods sold (COGS), and overhead. I threw in volume as well, which has less bottom-line impact than raising prices but still makes a difference, indicating that even the smallest of adjustments to any of these drivers can have big impact on the ultimate bottom line: net income.

Power of One Financial Drivers

As a reminder, the full list of Power of One financial drivers are:

Power of One Drivers:

- Price

- Volume

- Cost of Goods Sold (COGS)

- Accounts Receivables (A/R)

- Accounts Payable (A/P)

- Inventory (Turns)

- Overhead Expense

Here's how the other financial drivers produce bottom-line impact.

Accounts Receivable: Your accounts receivable are the bills you have sent clients that have not yet been paid. Your accounts receivable aging is the time between the date you bill your customer and the date you receive payment. I talked about the hospital that was able to shorten their accounts receivable aging by forty-eight days, with each day generating $200,000 in cash. Your daily accounts receivable may not be of that size, but every day that payment is delayed is a day the cash is not in your bank. Many companies have used simple techniques to accelerate payments from their customers.

If you mail your invoices, consider switching to email, saving the days those invoices would otherwise be in transit. Many customers prefer automatic ACH payments or credit card payments, both of which can shorten accounts receivable aging.

Accounts Payable: Like your accounts receivable, the bills you pay have an aging as well. Many invoices allow you to pay ten or thirty days after the date of the invoice. Many companies like to pay their bills the day they come in. Honorable, but your vendor says on the invoice that you can pay in ten or thirty days, why not keep your cash in the bank as long as possible? Some suppliers are willing to give longer terms for larger orders. When you take advantage of that window, you are essentially using your supplier's cash to fuel your business—and that's not a bad thing.

Inventory: I like to ask clients to see the inventory they have sitting on the shelf as stacks of dollar bills. If we can cut the inventory in half without reducing our output, half of that stack of cash can go back in the bank. Most have heard of the concept of just-in-time inventory: that when the input or inventory is there just as you need an input to make your widget, not before. That means there isn't any inventory—or stacks of cash—sitting on the shelf. Just-in-time inventory can be accomplished by better managing your cycle or negotiating with your input supplier to deliver inventory as necessary, rather than far in advance. And remember, inventory can also be intangible, for Professional Services firms, billable hours are very perishable, value-based inventory — if not used, that hour of inventory is gone. Is your intangible inventory well utilized?

Cash Forecast: As you sharpen your cash-finding skills, consider building a cash forecast. This might be as simple as a total cash-in-bank goal, but could also include an annual cash impact savings goal for each step in your Cash Conversion Cycle. The person who is accountable for the functional step in the process would be accountable for achieving the cash savings for that function. Accountability drives focus, which drives results.

You Don't Have to Go It Alone

If you're not sure where to start, you're not alone. It's hard to identify where to make change in your business on your own. After all, you're in the trenches all day every day, making it hard to see the forest for the trees. That's why a coach can be such a valuable investment.

Your Gravitas Impact Premium Coach is trained to help you find cash in your business. They can bring a fresh set of eyes to your review, enabling you to unearth hiccups in current processes, ask questions you hadn't considered yourself, and see areas for growth you wouldn't have noticed otherwise.

What if you work in a highly specialized field, with a unique set of challenges and opportunities? A coach doesn't need to have experience in your industry to be helpful. The superpower of a coach isn't industry experience; it's having a perspective that differs from your own. In fact, their lack of experience in a particular area can be a real asset.

One of my clients is a contractor. Prior to our collaboration, he was stuck, unable to find new ways to increase business. "You have 150 years of construction experience in your office," I told him. "You need someone who isn't in the industry—someone to ask the kinds of questions that might seem dumb; the stuff you've stopped asking because you know your business." That's what coaches do.

I used to think people called on me for the answers. Now I'm quite sure they hire me for the questions. Often, that outside perspective—those probing questions—is just what businesses need to reach new heights. In fact, my clients often have the right answers; the issue is finding it among the baggage they have accumulated over years and years in their business or industry.

My clients also tend to find that the answer doesn't appear right away. The reality is it's usually not the first one you come up with. A photographer wouldn't just take one snapshot when hoping to land the cover of National Geographic. An architect doesn't design a skyscraper in a single drawing. Assuming you'll arrive at the right answer right out of the gate follows the same flawed logic. Most people can't address their business's issues or find growth by landing upon and running with a single idea. A coach will help you get past that first idea or two to arrive at the next right one, and to implement it effectively to make a real difference in your operation.

I'll remind you of the powerful impact of working with a coach. My client that doubled their business in three years had fiddled around with a dozen different initiatives without any change to their top or bottom line. In a single coaching session, they were able to land on the one thing that would have the biggest impact on their business—and on their lives. The rest is history.

Rarely is an investment in a professional coach not a cash multiplier. You just can't achieve the same perspective from inside your operation. No sports team would ever consider competing at any level without a coach present to help them through—whether it's a middle school baseball team or a world-class professional team. What makes you think you could compete in your marketplace without one? Whether you see yourself as world class already, or you just want to be, you need a coach.

There are a number of ways to access the benefits of Gravitas Impact, from online tools to the opportunity to work one-on-one with a coach who can help you find those nickels in the niches to fuel your economic engine. Visit **GravitasImpact.com** today to learn more.

KEY POINTS:

Cash, The Fuel For Your Economic Engine: Using the *Cash Conversion Cycle Worksheet,* I outlined how you can accelerate, and increase, your cash flow through shortening time, eliminating waste and mistakes and changing your business process or model. Through the *How 1+1+1=19* exercise, I demonstrated that you can—and should—find cash within your operations to fuel your economic engine.

You Don't Have to Go It Alone: Your Gravitas Impact Premium Coach is trained to help you find cash in your business. They can bring a fresh set of eyes to your review, enabling you to unearth hiccups in current processes, ask questions you hadn't considered yourself, and see areas for growth you wouldn't have noticed otherwise.

DOWNLOAD YOUR FREE

PROFIT TOOLS AT

www.GravitasImpact.com/FuelYourEngine

Notes

1 - Collins, J. C. (2009). How the mighty fall: and why some companies never give in. New York: HarperCollins Publishers.

2 - Churchill, N. C., & Mullins, J. C. (2014, August 1). How Fast Can Your Company Afford to Grow? Retrieved from https://hbr.org/2001/05/how-fast-can-your-company-afford-to-grow

3 - Miltz, Allen, Milner, Josh & Lokot, Tim. Cash Flow Story. https://www.cashflowstory.com/

Recommended Reading:

Simple Numbers, Straight Talk, Big Profits!, Greg Crabtree: Take the mystery out of small business finance with this no-frills guide to understanding the numbers that will guide your business out of any financial black hole.

The Customer Funded Business, John Mullins, PhD: Uncover five novel approaches that scrappy and innovative 21st century entrepreneurs working in companies large and small have ingeniously adapted from their predecessors.

Profit First, Mike Michalowicz: A simple, counterintuitive cash management solution that will help small businesses break out of the doom spiral and achieve instant profitability.

Your Business Is A Leaky Bucket, Howard M Shore: Using the metaphor of a "Leaky Bucket," Howard Shore addresses the 15 most common issues in the areas of people, strategy, and execution that drain energy, direction, and profitability from every business.

ABOUT THE AUTHOR:

Jeffrey A. Redmon helps his clients safely achieve their business goals by leveraging his knowledge, experience and networks to each client's advantage. Through practical advice, he challenges his clients to bring clarity to their vision, objectives and strategies. Jeff is founder and principal of Redmon Law Chartered, with 30 years of engagement as a trusted legal advisor to business owners on general counsel matters and commercial real estate.

Jeff is a leader of Inner Circle groups, where business owners on a monthly basis can share and get feedback from other business owners. He is a tireless volunteer for many nonprofit organizations but has a passion for helping youth reach their full potential. Jeff has served on his local school board for 22 years and been an active volunteer for the Girl Scouts for 35 years. Jeff currently serves on his local Girl Scout Council Board as treasurer and served two terms on the National Board of the Girl Scouts of the USA. For nearly 25 years, he served as a volunteer board development and finance consultant, working with Girl Scout Councils across the United States.

He is an active member of Gravitas Impact Premium Coaches, a mentor to coaches worldwide, and a valued contributor to programs and content for their global ecosystem.

CONTACT JEFF: jredmon@redmonlaw.com — www.RedmonLaw.com

Adam Siegel is a trusted advisor for willing CEOs and their leadership teams who want to successfully scale their business. With his business, Visage Growth Partners, he demystifies growth by combining a proven, simple and practical methodology with his 20+ years of corporate executive leadership experiences across a diverse set of industries as part of the Gravitas Impact community.

CONTACT ADAM: adam@visagegp.com - www.visagegrowthpartners.com

ABOUT GRAVITAS IMPACT:

WHO WE ARE:

Gravitas Impact is a vibrant community of experienced business coaches across the globe devoted to helping you achieve your extraordinary goals.

WHAT WE DO:

Gravitas Impact pairs companies with the most experienced, effective executive coaches in the world. Our coaches use time-tested tools and concepts to guide leadership and executive teams towards dramatically improving their organizational performance, revenue and culture.

Our coaches and their clients appreciate knowing that we set a high bar for acceptance into our organization. These premium coaches bring their clients the most current and incisive expertise, based on constantly updated insights and tools from our events, trainings and network of faculty thought leaders. From world-class intellectual property in multiple languages, to time-tested growth concepts and tools, Gravitas Impact offers coaches access to ongoing, continuous education and training in tools from thought leaders and guest speakers.

BECOME A COACH: www.GravitasImpact.com/Apply

FIND A COACH: www.GravitasImpact.com/Hire

BEST COMMUNITY – BEST LEARNING – BEST TOOLS

Made in the USA
Middletown, DE
29 May 2020

96220073R00033